Old Kyoto
A Short Social History

TITLES IN THE SERIES

Series Editors, China Titles:
NIGEL CAMERON, SYLVIA FRASER-LU

Old Kyoto

A Short Social History

JOHN LOWE

OXFORD
UNIVERSITY PRESS

OXFORD
UNIVERSITY PRESS

Oxford University Press is a department of the University of Oxford.
It furthers the University's objective of excellence in research, scholarship,
and education by publishing worldwide in

Oxford New York

Athens Auckland Bangkok Bogotá Buenos Aires Calcutta
Cape Town Chennai Dar es Salaam Delhi Florence Hong Kong Istanbul
Karachi Kuala Lumpur Madrid Melbourne Mexico City Mumbai
Nairobi Paris São Paulo Shanghai Singapore Taipei Tokyo Toronto Warsaw

with associated companies in Berlin Ibadan

Oxford is a registered trade mark of Oxford University Press

Published in the United States
by Oxford University Press Inc., New York

© Oxford University Press 2000

First published 2000
This impression (lowest digit)
1 3 5 7 9 10 8 6 4 2

British Library Cataloguing in Publication Data
available

Library of Congress Cataloging-in-Publication Data
available

ISBN 0-19-590940-2

Printed in Hong Kong
Published by Oxford University Press (China) Ltd
18th Floor, Warwick House East, Taikoo Place, 979 King's Road, Quarry Bay
Hong Kong

In affectionate memory of my friend Philip Hofer

Acknowledgements

I first visited Kyoto thirty-five years ago and I have visited the city nearly every year since then, including living there for twelve years. I spent much of that time sightseeing in the city and its surroundings, but with the enormous number of temples, shrines, gardens, monuments, and festivals, I failed to see everything. Kyoto's history is as complex as its historical remains, and in this small book I have only tried to give a glimpse of the social life at different periods. I hope that such a slight treatment will give the reader an idea of the diverse life of this ancient capital and, even better, tempt readers to visit the city for themselves. My knowledge of Kyoto is based on the advice and help I received over the years from both Japanese and foreigners living in Kyoto, and I offer them my thanks. They are too numerous to list here, but my gratitude is none the less for that.

I am grateful to the following people and institutions who have allowed me to reproduce their works of art and, where necessary, supplied photographs: the Pitt Rivers Museum, Oxford University, and their photographer Malcolm Osman; Jingo-ji Temple, Kyoto; Museum of the Imperial Collections, Tokyo; Tokyo National Museum; Kyoto Museum of Archaeology; Lutz Dille; Harumi Isobe; and Clifton Karhu. Other photographs were taken by the author.

With the exception of the samurai armour and the Noh mask, all the other objects from the Pitt Rivers Museum are part of a gift of Japanese arts and crafts the author made to the museum in 1996.

The endpapers show scenes of Kyoto life, taken from a pair of eighteenth-century screens. Formerly in the author's collection.

Contents

Introduction

The Japanese history covered in this book—the Heian period (794–1185) through to the Edo period (1600–1868)—is complicated. The character of its institutions, its social structure, and its religions and culture have no parallels in the West, making it difficult for the Western reader to absorb. This is compounded by the necessary condensation in this brief account, and the complexity of Japanese names.

From earliest times the emperor, both ruler and Shinto deity descended from the Sun Goddess, was at the centre of Japanese life. History records 124 emperors (including eight empresses), beginning with fourteen legendary emperors, drawn from Shinto mythology. The emperor remained a divine being until Emperor Hirohito renounced this status at the end of the Second World War in 1945.

Despite their divine nature, emperors were often treated as no more than pawns in the political game. The great Fujiwara family, while outwardly paying respect, manipulated the imperial succession to increase its own power. Frequent changes of fortune notwithstanding, the Japanese imperial throne survived to become the oldest in the world.

Shinto is the indigenous religion of Japan, rooted in an ancient rural nature worship in which every natural object houses a god. Different, complex theologies are followed by different branches of Shinto. Each of the great shrines, of which there are several in Kyoto, follows its own beliefs with its own style of architecture and its own festivals.

Buddhism was adopted from China as Japan's official religion in the early eighth century. China exercised the deepest influence over Japan: contact was maintained by a series of embassies between the two countries, which continued until the late ninth century. After this, Chinese influence continued for centuries. With Buddhism came Confucianism and Taoism and, most important, the adoption by the Japanese of the Chinese written language. The influence of China had the most profound effect on every element of Japanese life. Buddhism was eagerly adopted by the court, who added its colourful rituals to their already highly ritualized court life. Wherever one looks—in religion, arts, and politics—one sees the influence of China. New phonetic alphabets were devised to enable the Chinese characters to fit Japanese grammar. And as late as the seventeenth century, the Tokugawas created neo-Confucianism, to give their government the voice of traditional authority.

This brief social history shows how the supreme powers of the emperor, so skillfully exercised by Emperor Kammu, were first eroded by the nobility, then later and more openly by the rise of the warrior class, supported by their mercenary soldiers, the samurai. In the Muromachi period, the Ashikaga paid lip service to the emperor, but openly became the supreme rulers of Japan, all powerful in war and politics.

The shogunate continued to rule Japan until it was overthrown in 1868 by the supporters of the Meiji restoration. The long Edo period saw the emergence of an increasingly wealthy merchant class, who created a new culture to suit their own tastes. Theirs was the world of pleasure, 'the floating world' of the geisha quarters, the kabuki theatre, the magnificent woodblock prints; a world of indulgence and often licentiousness. Thus, at each period, a different class of society brought about great changes and left its individual mark on Japanese social history.

During the Heian period, the capital was called Heian-kyo, a name chosen by Emperor Kammu. I have followed historical precedent, changing the name of the capital to Kyoto when this title was first introduced in the eleventh century.

1

The Imperial Way:
The Founding of Heian-kyo 794

Emperor Kammu (737–806) founded his new capital, Heian-
kyo, in 794. Officially called Kyoto since the eleventh
century, it remained the capital of Japan until 1868. Kammu,
the fiftieth emperor of Japan (if one includes the fourteen
legendary rulers who head the official list), is generally
regarded as one of its four greatest rulers, noted for his energy,
administrative ability, and enthusiasm for scholarship. He
was the eldest son of Emperor Konin; his mother was a low-
ranking secondary consort of Korean origin. Kammu had
proved himself an able administrator as rector of the
university in Nara, the previous capital, but it was only
through the efforts of his father-in-law, the court official
Fujiwara no Momokawa, that he succeeded as Crown prince
in 772, aged thirty-four.

Emperor Kammu, who ascended the imperial throne in
781, was the only Japanese emperor to rule from three
capitals. Previously, each emperor had built a new capital, a
practice brought to an end by cost and inconvenience. When
Kammu became emperor, he was aware that the Nara court
was dominated by the priests of its powerful Buddhist
temples, who increasingly interfered with the politics and
economy of the government. The power of the priests had
reached such a state that in 769 the powerful Buddhist priest,
Dokyo, had plotted unsuccessfully to become emperor.
Kammu was old enough to remember the incident, which
may have prompted him to move the capital from Nara after
his enthronement. He ruled in Nara for three years before
he took steps to build a new capital to the north at Nagaoka.

The new capital lasted only ten years (784–794), falling prey to court intrigue, superstition, and murder. These misfortunes prompted Kammu to consider abandoning Nagaoka and to find another site for the capital—a serious measure considering the cost Nagaoka had already placed on the imperial finances.

A court official, Wake no Kiyomaro, took the lead in urging the emperor to find a new site. Kiyomaro was generally admired for the courage he had shown during the Dokyo incident. It is recorded that in March 792, probably encouraged by Kiyomaro, Emperor Kammu went to inspect a potential site for a new capital under the pretext of going on a hunting expedition. Further hunting trips provided opportunities for surveying other sites to the north, and in January 793, an official party was sent openly to survey the land around the village of Uda, on the north-western outskirts of modern Kyoto. This expedition marks the real beginning of Heian-kyo. Only six days later, the emperor moved out of his palace at Nagaoka, so that it could be dismantled for its removal to the new capital.

Emperor Kammu had depended on financial assistance from the Hata family for the building of Nagaoka. This family were to contribute even more generously, with money, land, and labour, to the building of the larger Heian-kyo. The Hata clan were descended from Korean immigrants who had settled in central Japan around AD 400, and by the beginning of the Heian period had been completely assimilated into Japanese society. With their skills in irrigation, sericulture, and weaving (*hata* means loom in Japanese) they had acquired wealth, land, and position. An important branch of the Hata family had settled in the Kyoto basin (Plate 1), and the family also established important Shinto shrines in the Kyoto area. By Emperor Kammu's time, the main Hata family were extremely wealthy, and had close ties with the imperial court.

There is no precise evidence about the contribution the Hatas made to the creation of Heian-kyo but, as with everything to do with the new capital, one must piece together fragmentary historical records and traditional hearsay. Without question, the Hatas had contributed money for the construction of Nagaoka. The Chief Officer of Works at the start of Heian-kyo was Oguromaro, whose wife was the daughter of Hata no Imiki Shimamaro, who had been raised to the lower fourth rank at the imperial court. There can be little doubt that Shimamaro had inherited the wealth of the Hata family and, as head of the Hata clan in this region, owned the land that was to provide the site of Heian-kyo. One contemporary document states that the palace was built on the site of the Hata's house. All these arrangements must have been known to the emperor, although there is no record of any inducements, such as promotion at court, being offered to the Hata family. But, there were obvious advantages in serving the needs of the emperor and securing the new capital in the heart of their own lands.

Emperor Kammu must have been relieved to have found a site for a new capital which released him from the ill-fated Nagaoka. There is a fragment of an edict he issued in 795, which shows his appreciation of the beauty of the new site and, typical of his practical character, its accessibility for his people: 'The mountains and rivers of the great palace of Kadzuno are beautiful, and it is convenient for the peasants of all the provinces.'

The site of Heian-kyo was beautiful and, despite the growth and urbanization of modern Kyoto, remains so today. The long valley is surrounded east, west, and north by wooded hills and mountains (Plate 2). To the south the valley opens out to a broad plain stretching away to Osaka and the sea. From north to south, the Katsura River runs on the western side, and the Kamogawa River to the east (Fig. 1.1).

3

1.1 The Kamogawa River, Roger Nicholson, 1982.

Roughly speaking, these two rivers formed the eastern and western boundaries of Heian-kyo. It was long thought that the Kamogawa River originally flowed through part of the site of Heian-kyo, and had to be diverted. Recent archaeological excavations revealed a massive subterranean wall of rock that could not have been penetrated in early Heian times to allow the redirection of the river, which must, more or less, have followed its present course.

To the north-east of the valley, traditionally the direction from which evil influences came, stood the highest mountain, Mount Hiei, blocking 'the devil's mouth'. All the physical features surrounding the site were auspicious and in accord with the requirements of Chinese geomancy. The emperor and the court approved: the removal of the capital was reported to the gods at Ise and other major shrines, and work began in 793. At a meeting of poets, the name of Heian-kyo was chosen for the new city, 'Capital of Peace and Tranquillity'.

The emperor and his court were still deeply influenced by China. The new capital, like its three predecessors, was modelled on the great T'ang capital Chang'an, modern Xian. Heian-kyo was to be larger and grander than Fujiwara, Nara, and Nagaoka, though considerably smaller than Chang'an.

The rectangular site of Heian-kyo was about 3.1 miles from north to south, and 2.8 miles from east to west. The four boundary roads were enclosed by a low wall, with canals running down the middle. Excluding the boundary roads, eleven wide avenues ran north to south and east to west. These were all linked by smaller roads running in the same directions—the city laid out in a chequerboard pattern.

In the centre of the northern part of the city was the Daidairi, the Great Palace Enclosure, which contained the emperor's quarters and the most important ceremonial buildings. From the southern gate of the Daidairi stretched the great avenue, Suzaku-oji, eighty feet wide and lined with willows. It ran down through the centre of the city to meet the main southern gate, Rajo-mon, made famous to the Western world in the film *Rashomon*. This avenue divided the capital into Ukyo (the Right Capital) and Sakyo (the Left Capital).

Outside the Great Palace Enclosure, official premises mingled with domestic dwellings, seniority at court dictating the nearness of one's house to the palace, and the size of the plot of land allocated for building. In the southern half of the city were the large eastern and western markets, two guest houses for foreign embassies, and three prisons. It has been estimated that by 794 the capital contained 80,000 houses, with a population of about 400,000. Even allowing for the fact that many of the buildings at Nagaoka had been dismantled and brought to the new capital, Heian-kyo had been built with remarkable speed. The existing documents make little reference to the scale of the construction. There is one edict instructing nine families from different provinces to be responsible for the construction of a number of the city gates, and in a later document it is recorded that 24,000 workmen were drafted from various provinces by the Office of Works. Despite such early achievements, building continued for many years.

Emperor Kammu had left Nara with the prime purpose of freeing his government from the interference of the great Buddhist temples. He had no intention of recreating this situation in Heian-kyo, but he was a devout Buddhist, and he allowed two temples to be built on its southern boundary for the protection of the capital. The temples Sai-ji and To-ji (Fig. 1.2), on either side of the great southern gate, Rajo-mon, protected the left and right sides of the capital. Sai-ji was

1.2 To-ji, one of Heian-kyo's temples.

6

completely destroyed—probably burnt—at an unknown date and nothing remains but a few foundation stones. In 823, To-ji was given by Emperor Saga to Kobo Daishi, Japan's greatest and most popular Buddhist saint, and this large temple remains the centre of the Shingon sect in Kyoto, its tall pagoda rising just south of Kyoto station. There were Shinto shrines within the Great Palace Enclosure, but otherwise there were no other religious buildings in the capital.

Although Emperor Kammu has long been recognized as one of the great rulers of Japan, little is known of his personal character or his daily life, and no contemporary portrait exists. He lived until he was sixty-nine and had thirty-six children. Apart from creating two new capitals, he showed great energy in ruling the country. Anxious to unify Japan, he appointed Sakanoue no Tamuramaro commander-in-chief and sent him with an army of 40,000 men to subdue the Ainu, the indigenous people who lived in northern Japan. The expedition was successful but imposed a further burden on Emperor Kammu's treasury. To improve his financial situation, he reformed the provincial administrative system and sent officials to audit the tax registers. He pursued schemes for improving the water supply, an interest reflected in the many canals running along the streets of Heian-kyo, whose water was drawn from the two counties of Atago and Kadzuno. Despite his administrative responsibilities, he was a great scholar and particularly encouraged Chinese scholarship. Although he had opposed the Buddhist establishment in Nara, he was a generous patron of the monks Saicho and Kobo Daishi, who introduced new Buddhist sects from China. His achievements brought great power and prestige to the throne of Japan.

Thereafter, one can only deduce the day-to-day lifestyle of the emperor from a few fragmentary documents, and from those parts of Heian-kyo which provided the setting for his ceremonial life, solemn rituals, and rarer moments of relaxation, interspersed with official banquets and formal processions. Within the Great Palace Enclosure were the Imperial Residence, the Dairi, and the Chodo-in, an inner enclosure containing the eight great departments of state, and at the north end, the principal hall of state, the Daigoku-den. Although all these buildings were destroyed long ago, replicas, two-thirds the size of some of the original buildings, were reconstructed to form Kyoto's Heian Shrine in commemoration of the eleven-hundredth anniversary of the founding of Heian-kyo in 1894. The great entrance gate to the shrine (Fig. 1.3) is a replica of the Oten Gate, originally the south entrance to the Chodo-in. The main shrine building, painted vermilion in the Chinese style, like the gate, is a replica of the great hall of state. It is raised above the ground and a flight of steps leads up to the row of columns which front the building (Plate 3); wings stretch out on either

1.3 The entrance gateway of the Heian Shrine.

side and turn to end in the Blue Dragon tower on the east, the White Tiger tower on the west. The rebuilt Daigoku-den was burnt down in 1976 and was reconstructed three years later. The modern Heian Shrine gives some idea of the magnificence of the ceremonial buildings of Heian-kyo that provided the setting for the unending rituals in which the emperor was the central figure. It is difficult to imagine the splendour of the Great Palace Enclosure, with some one hundred buildings, but though smaller, the shrine calls to mind the Forbidden City in Beijing, which also served the Chinese imperial court.

One should not presume that Kammu was a prisoner within this ritualized life. He was an unusually successful and strong ruler served, but never dominated, by the able men who carried out his policies. Contemporary records indicate that he took pride and a close interest in the development of his new capital, making frequent tours of inspection, looking after the interests of the peasants who lost their rice fields when the city was built, and visiting various aristocratic homes, 'where he bestowed robes on those of the fifth rank and over'. Four days after he took up residence in the capital, 'The officials of the Office of Works and the Kuni no Miyakko (an imperial prince) presented offerings and congratulations on the change of capital, and the Emperor bestowed robes, umbrellas, and produce on those of the fifth rank and over.' There were banquets for ministers with dancing, music, and poems, and on one excursion, the emperor announced that 'our heart has been touched by the suffering at the prison of Horikawa. Now, therefore, we declare an amnesty'. The emperor was concerned for his humblest subjects.

At last, in February 796, the Daigoku-den was finished, and the emperor was able to ascend the imperial throne and hold court for the first time in Heian-kyo, followed by a banquet and the bestowing of robes. As with everything, there were strict rules controlling imperial banquets, derived from Chinese practices. The dishes might have included salted jellyfish and sea squirt; carp or sea bream marinated in vinegar; steamed brown rice; nuts and fruits; and Chinese-style confectionery. Food was served cold and all the dishes were placed on the table together. Great attention was paid to the appearance of the food, a feature of Japanese cuisine which has come down to the present day.

Almost the last documentary reference reports that 'the Emperor made a tour of inspection of the city, and finally went to the Shinsen-en' (Plate 4). This was the 'divine spring garden', a thirty-three-acre imperial pleasure ground, below the south-eastern corner of the Great Palace Enclosure. Miraculously, a small part of this garden still exists today— the only genuine remnant of Heian-kyo, immediately south of Nijo Castle. All that remains is an attractive lake and, at the southern shore, some small and modern Shinto shrines. But it is a peaceful oasis in the heart of the city.

The Great Palace Enclosure had no proper gardens—only tubs here and there, containing cherry, plum, wisteria, and other small trees in the Chinese taste. The Shinsen-en was a popular summer retreat for Emperor Kammu and his successors, until it fell into disrepair during the fifteenth century. Richard Ponsonby Fane describes the various activities that the emperor and his courtiers enjoyed there: 'Entertainments of all kinds were arranged, banquets were given, and poem-parties; the literati assembled to construct Chinese odes; wrestling matches and military exercises were witnessed, and fishing was indulged in in the lakes. There are innumerable references in old poems to the beauties of the place and the amusements held there.'

Emperor Kammu died in 806 and was buried to the south of Heian-kyo, in the neighbourhood of Momoyama. In time, the whereabouts of his tomb became uncertain, and eventually another tomb was created for him near the tomb of Emperor Meiji. When the Heian Shrine was rebuilt in 1894, the spirits of Emperor Kammu and Emperor Komei, the first and last emperors to rule in the capital of Kyoto, were enshrined here; a fitting resting place for this great emperor and founder of the ancient capital.

2

Court Life in Heian-kyo:
The Fujiwara Period 967–1068

The Fujiwara family's influence at the imperial court dates back to the seventh century, when Fujiwara no Kamatari helped the imperial family to destroy the Soga family, who had tried to seize the government. During the next three centuries the Fujiwaras consolidated their influence by marrying their daughters to reigning and future emperors. In 866, Fujiwara no Yoshifusa was appointed regent, the first time in Japanese history that someone not of imperial blood had occupied this office. The Fujiwaras never attempted to place a male member of their family on the throne but, by the marriage of their daughters, they gained a tight control over the imperial household. In 887 they created the new post of Minister, allowing a Fujiwara to hold this high office. By 967, and for the next hundred years, their power and the wealth from their estates was unrivalled. Fujiwara no Michinaga (966–1028) dominated the court for more than thirty years and was the father of four empresses and grandfather of three emperors. He epitomized Fujiwara influence, and he ruled over a court of exceptional brilliance—a great age of Japanese culture and literature. It is this literature that gives us such a vivid and detailed picture of court life of this period.

One other date is important in understanding the life of the Fujiwara period. In 894, the official embassy to China was cancelled and not revived. Chinese influence over the court continued, but direct influence weakened, and Japan began the long process of Japanizing its many Chinese elements. This process was already apparent in the building of Heian-kyo, where although the official buildings were in a Chinese style, domestic architecture had a Japanese character. But the severance of direct contact with the Mainland isolated Japan, and this isolation marks the culture of the Fujiwara period: Heian-kyo became a world set apart.

The Fujiwara period is now best remembered for its brilliant literature, fiction, and diaries, mostly written by court ladies, and providing a detailed account of the social life of the nobility of Heian-kyo. Murasaki Shikibu's *Tale of Genji*, written early in the eleventh century, is the world's first novel and a great Japanese literary classic. A more precise account of contemporary court life is found in Sei Shonagon's (fl. late tenth century) *Pillow Book*, a collection of her thoughts and observations on a great variety of subjects, from the beauty of the seasons to the correct behaviour of lovers. There are other important contemporary writings, prose and poetry, nearly all written by women. Murasaki Shikibu also kept a diary for two years, and a collection of 123 poems are preserved, though not all by her. There is Lady Sarashina's diary, and a novel written by Murasaki Shikibu's daughter.

There are several reasons why women writers excelled at this time. The men of the Heian court, if hardly busy, were more involved than the court ladies in the endless rituals which occupied the life of the imperial court. Courtiers may have looked down on the writing of novels and diaries as an effeminate occupation. More important, however, was the introduction of a phonetic script (*kana*), sometimes called 'women's writing'. Women were forbidden, or at least discouraged, from learning the Chinese characters, the official language of the court. The *kana* syllables enabled a closeness to the Japanese language, and new perspectives in literature which the women writers were quick to exploit.

Remarkably little is known of the life of Murasaki Shikibu, and both her life and her work continue to be the subject of scholarly debate. She was born in the 970s into a branch of the Fujiwara family. She was brought up by a cultured father, and may have been able to share the study of the Chinese and Japanese classics with her elder brother. Rather late, when she was about twenty, she was married to a relation much older than her. He died in 1001, and we know that she had a daughter. Her husband and family are not mentioned in her diary. In 1004, her father was appointed governor of the province of Echizen, about eighty miles from Heian, and Murasaki Shikibu became a maid of honour to the consort of Emperor Ichijo. Murasaki Shikibu's diary, begun in 1008, gives no dates and is largely impressionistic. Nothing is known of her final years, the date of her death, or exactly when she wrote *The Tale of Genji*. It is obvious, however, that her life at court provided the background and models for several characters in her novel. While the modern reader may find *The Tale of Genji* slow, lacking in dramatic incident, and cumbersome in its courtly language, in all of these things it is a perfect reflection of the court life of Heian-kyo in Murasaki Shikibu's lifetime. This is what makes the novel such a valuable document of Heian social history.

Genji is the son of the emperor by his most favoured concubine. His mother dies, a victim of the jealousy and malice of the court ladies. Genji grows up the idealized prince and first marries Aoi, but a great part of the book describes his numerous love affairs, which culminate in his union with Murasaki Shikibu, a heroine fully worthy of him. He dies at the age of fifty-one, and the last ten books of the novel are chiefly concerned with Kaoru, wrongly thought by the court to be Genji's son.

Sei Shonagon's *Pillow Book*, though giving a more fragmentary view of court life, is more direct in both style and observations, yet Sei Shonagon also writes some beautiful, poetic descriptions. She is not as great a writer as Murasaki Shikibu, but she is more accessible. Her *Pillow Book* is an unusual literary form, where her jottings vary greatly in length from one line to a few pages, and deal with anything that catches her eye or comes into her head.

Almost nothing is known about Sei Shonagon. She was born about 965, the daughter of a provincial official of the Kiyowara clan, who had a reputation as a scholar and a poet. She served as a lady-in-waiting to Empress Sadako in the late tenth century, but nothing is known of her life after the end of her service at court. It is said that she died in loneliness and poverty. She may have been married briefly, but the facts are obscure.

She was known to Murasaki Shikibu, who wrote somewhat maliciously in her diary:

Sei Shonagon has the most extraordinary air of self-satisfaction. . . . Someone who makes such an effort to be different from others is bound to fall in people's esteem, and I can only think that her future will be a hard one. She is a gifted woman, to be sure, yet, if one gives free rein to one's emotions even under the most inappropriate circumstances, if one has to sample each interesting thing that comes along, people are bound to regard one as frivolous. And how can things turn out well for such a woman? (Translated by Ivan Morris.)

The two women served as ladies-in-waiting at rival courts, and some of the entries in *The Pillow Book* do suggest that Sei Shonagon had a sharp tongue, and a certain malice that no doubt was not confined to her writing. But whatever her imperfections, she was 'a gifted woman'. There we may agree with Murasaki Shikibu.

There are 185 separate entries in *The Pillow Book*, and nearly every one of them throws some light on the life of that time. Sei Shonagon enjoyed compiling lists, often two consecutive lists cataloguing favourable and unfavourable objects or occasions. 'Things That Give a Clean Feeling', such as a new metal bowl or a rush mat, are contrasted with 'Things That Give an Unclean Feeling', a rat's nest, children who sniffle, or faded clothes. There are several entries which describe the qualities of each season, and here Sei Shonagon is at her most poetic. Anybody who has ever spent a hot and humid day in Kyoto will recognize the pleasures of falling darkness in her 123rd entry, 'During the Hot Months':

During the hot months it is a great delight to sit on the veranda, enjoying the cool of the evening and observing how the outlines of objects gradually become blurred. At such a moment I particularly enjoy the sight of a gentleman's carriage, preceded by outriders clearing the way. Sometimes a couple of commoners will pass in a carriage with the rear blinds slightly raised. As the oxen trot along, one has a pleasant sense of freshness. It is still more delightful when the sound of a lute or a flute comes from inside the carriage, and one feels sorry when it disappears in the distance. Occasionally one catches a whiff of the oxen's leather cruppers; it is a strange, unfamiliar smell, but, absurd as it may seem, I find something rather pleasant about it.

On a very dark night it is delightful when the aroma of smoke from the pine-torches at the head of a procession is wafted through the air and pervades the carriage in which one is travelling. (Translated by Ivan Morris.)

Sei Shonagon, by such vignettes, evokes scenes over one thousand years old. While Murasaki Shikibu brilliantly creates the mood of the Heian court, Sei Shonagon is unerring in supplying the details.

Since the founding of the capital and the beginning of the Fujiwara period, Heian-kyo had undergone one major change. Unlike many major cities, it expanded to the east. Today the urbanization has even crept up the lower slopes of the eastern mountains. The western half of Heian-kyo did not flourish. The western market was closed, buildings fell into disrepair, and open ground originally set aside for further building instead became a neglected undergrowth, the haunt of vagrants and robbers, and avoided by honest citizens. The eastern half of the city, and the streets immediately around the imperial enclosure, flourished, and the villas of the highest nobles were sited as near to the palace as possible. The amount of land allotted to members of the nobility also depended on their rank, and hence the size of their houses.

All the villas of the nobility, whatever the owner's rank, shared a common form of architecture. This was the Shinden style, which took its name from the central hall of the complex, whose basic plan varied according to the rank and wealth of the owner. The main hall, the living quarters of the owner, was linked by covered corridors to smaller halls housing the family members and their servants, and the necessary offices.

The Shinden style was Japanese, uninfluenced by Chinese architecture. The villas were built of wood, the buildings raised about one foot above the ground. The roofs had deep eaves and were covered with bark shingles or wattle, cooler for summer than tiles. The complex, which could cover 3.5 acres or more, faced south over a courtyard where ceremonies and entertainment were held. Beyond was a large garden pond, with an island reached by bridges. Two covered corridors ran south from the main complex, ending by the pond in small 'fishing' or 'fountain' pavilions. The island and surroundings of the pond were planted with trees, shrubs, and flowers, the whole area enclosed by thick earth walls capped by tiles. Such villas provide much of the background to the action in *The Tale of Genji*.

These villas must have been reasonably pleasant in summer, but bitterly cold in winter, with almost no privacy in any season. There were outer wooden shutters for the cold weather, and bamboo blinds for the summer. Within, the

17

women lived in a perpetual half-light, created by the screens and curtains they retreated behind in the presence of men, to ensure their privacy. The floors were bare wood—*tatami* was not widely used until the seventeenth century—and there were individual straw mats and cushions. In the main halls there was a curtained platform, 2 feet high and 9 feet square, surrounded by curtains. Within, there was a screened sleeping area, where the nobility slept in their clothes. The court ladies also retreated behind a frame hung with opaque curtains when talking to their male visitors.

Both Murasaki Shikibu and Sei Shonagon make it clear that ardent lovers had little difficulty making nocturnal visits to ladies in these villas. Screens and curtains offered little protection against amorous advances and, strange as it may seem, in the gloom and behind the concealment of the curtains, it was not unknown for a man to make love to the wrong woman. The error is more understandable when one remembers the perpetual dimness and that the lovers remained fully clothed: nakedness was unattractive to the Japanese for many centuries.

The dominant feature of Heian court life may have been boredom. The court attended an annual cycle of Shinto rites and Buddhist ceremonies, the latter more popular with the court ladies since they were more colourful. This tradition lingers on in modern Kyoto, which still has nine or ten festivals each month, some lasting several days, and some as old as Heian-kyo (Fig. 2.1).

Many of the nobility occupied official posts. A few were diligent, but most accepted the privileges without undertaking the responsibilities, thereby weakening the imperial government. The court ladies mostly lived out their lives in the gloom of their villas, finding a welcome change in court ceremonies and elaborate processions. Family life was extremely formal: family members only met on special

2.1 The Boat Festival (Mifune Matsuri, third Sunday in May) at Arashiyama.

occasions, otherwise living in separate parts of their villa, and a brother might never see his sister. The claustrophobia of life for both men and women is evident in *The Pillow Book*.

Heian-kyo had not only severed all relations with the outside world, but the nobility knew little, and cared less, for those parts of Japan more than a day's journey from the capital. For most of the men, and all of the women, the only form of transport was the lumbering ox-drawn carriage, whose elaborateness was dictated by rank, and which moved at a speed of two miles per hour (Fig. 2.2). The military and some others used horses, but the court's attitude to travel is illustrated in *The Tale of Genji*, where Prince Niou tells his lover that the rigours of the journey prevent him from visiting her at Uji, hardly ten miles south of the capital. It was this isolation which fostered the brilliant and unique culture of the Fujiwara period.

2.2 Nijo Tenno escaping from his palace in an ox-cart. *Heiji Monogatari,* thirteenth century. National Museum, Tokyo.

Daily life was dominated by an extraordinary mixture of religion and superstition. Shinto was the state religion, with a variety of taboos and superstitions drawn from shamanism and witchcraft. The court also followed both the Tendai and Shingon sects of Buddhism, but Amida Buddhism, salvation by faith alone, was becoming popular (Fig. 2.3). This new Buddhist cult is perfectly represented in the beautiful Phoenix Hall at Uji (Fig. 2.4), south of Kyoto, the only surviving building of this period. It was built by Fujiwara no Michinaga and his son, and a fine statue of the Amida was enshrined there in 1053. Apart from this great temple, it is clear that members of the court were fond of using the sect's mantra, 'I call on thee Amida Buddha', to ensure their salvation.

Confucianism influenced contemporary thought, enforcing family solidarity and filial piety, though Prince Genji and many real-life nobles ignored Confucian precepts. Taoism was a further strand in the beliefs of the court, but the most powerful element was superstition: avoiding bad

2.3 Standing figure of the Buddha of Healing, Fujiwara period. Pitt Rivers Museum, Oxford.

2.4 Phoenix Hall (Byodo-in), the villa of Fujiwara no Michinaga (966–1028).

21

directions; waiting for an auspicious day to cut one's nails; and only washing one's hair once every five days. Dreams were subject to careful analysis, and a journey, or even a battle might be postponed if the omens were inauspicious.

In this hierarchic society, rank was everything, and a high rank depended on relationships, above all with the Fujiwaras. The Heian aristocracy existed for itself, and hardly recognized the existence, or the rights, of anyone outside the ranks of the aristocracy. They regarded a posting to the provinces, even as governor, as being cast into outer darkness. Every detail of their lives, from the size of their houses to the decoration of their carriages, depended on their rank. Men might fall in love with low-ranking concubines, but they did not marry them.

Daily life was simple for a society so sophisticated in its culture. The nobility ate two main meals each day, at 10 a.m. and 4 p.m. When the first meal became later, a light breakfast was introduced. There seems to have been little interest in food, which may have been monotonous and poorly cooked. Correct etiquette at table was important. Sei Shonagon expressed horror at a group of carpenters she saw wolfing their food. The nobility were more interested in drinking a rice wine slightly less intoxicating than modern sake but strong enough to go to the heads of Heian courtiers. As in all things, drinking was surrounded by rituals. Cups of wine were floated in the water of the streams that ran through the villa gardens, and as each man or woman lifted a cup to drink, he or she had to invent or recite a fragment of poetry. Poems were central to many of the court pleasures and pastimes.

Many games enjoyed by the courtiers, both indoors and outdoors, are mentioned in contemporary literature. Go, a board game, had been introduced from China, and there was a form of backgammon, and dice games for gambling. There were literary games involving Chinese poems, and a great variety of games of comparison, from flowers and seashells to paintings, and detecting the identity of special incenses made to a private recipe. Outdoors, a court form of football, still to be seen in certain Japanese shrines, was popular, along with archery, sumo wrestling, and cock fighting, the only cruel sport of the time.

This way of life is perfectly portrayed in the rather impressionistic style of Murasaki Shikibu, which reflects an era when many people had only the vaguest sense of time, and an equally vague sense of their companions and lovers. Sei Shonagon is more down to earth and outspoken, and the two books, taken together, are perfectly complementary. Without them, we would know little of this great period of Japanese history.

3

Samurai Warriors and Zen Monks:
The Kamakura Period 1185–1392

The Heian period was brought to an end by the Kyoto government's failure to recognize the growing military power in the provinces of Japan. This situation became more serious during the Fujiwara period, when the court was wholly absorbed by ritual and high culture and became uninterested in anything taking place more than a few miles from the capital. The nobility often accepted provincial posts but never left Kyoto, leaving local officials, often warriors, to carry out their duties. Unwittingly, the emperors provided leaders for these provincial military clans.

The polygamous rulers produced too many sons, who confused the succession. They were stripped of their royal status, and were given the surnames of either Taira or Minamoto. Some of these men remained living in Kyoto as courtiers, while others accepted appointments in the provinces, where they settled. The Taira appear in the Kanto region (around modern Tokyo) from about 900; in the tenth and eleventh centuries the Minamoto became powerful warriors in Kanto and the northern provinces. In their armies the samurai were born.

The samurai, literally meaning 'one who serves', were elite warriors who emerged from the provinces from the early tenth century, and had become the ruling class by the twelfth century. The appearance of the samurai is usually dated from the warring clans of the Kanto region in the 930s, but there is no doubt that the number of true samurai increased during the second half of the Heian period. They remained the highest ranking citizens of Japan until their dissolution in the mid-1870s.

By the late eleventh century the Minamoto were the most powerful samurai clan north of Kanto. Their leader, Minamoto no Yoshiie, called 'First son of Hachiman the war god', was recognized as leader of all the samurai.

Kyoto, fearing Minamoto's power, began to favour the Taira, especially the retired emperors (*insei*) who were so influential in Kyoto politics from the eleventh century onwards. By the middle of the twelfth century, the Taira had gained power in the service of the retired emperors, while the Minamoto increased their influence at court under the patronage of the Fujiwara. Rivalry between the two clans grew tense in the capital. In the mid-twelfth century fighting broke out, nominally over the disputed succession, but in reality it opened a new age of samurai dominance that was to last until the beginning of the Meiji period in 1868.

By 1160, with the conflict called the Heiji Disturbance, battle lines were drawn and the Taira and Minamoto were at war with one another. In the first phase, the Taira triumphed but, becoming the new aristocracy, they made the old mistake of neglecting control of provincial power. In 1180, Minamoto chieftains started a new campaign which ended with the defeat of the Taira in 1185, at the sea battle of Dannoura, where the seven-year-old emperor was drowned and his mother Kenreimon'in was captured.

The victorious Minamoto no Yoritomo (Plate 5) realized that a new military government could only succeed away from the imperial intrigues of Kyoto, and in 1185 he established his seat of power at Kamakura, on the coast not far south of modern Tokyo, a place of old associations with his family. Power was transferred from the aristocracy to the samurai class, which took control of the private landed estates. The Kamakura administration assumed the right to appoint provincial officials, military governors, land stewards, and the authority to raise taxes. In 1192, the absolute power of Yoritomo was confirmed when he assumed the highest military title of shogun, or 'barbarian subduing generalissimo'.

In 1199, Yoritomo died and real power passed to the family of his widow, Hojo Masako. The Hojo family ruled as regents during most of the Kamakura period, since Yoritomo had eliminated the rivals in his own family. The Hojo family ruled firmly, and their rule was a period of peace, prosperity, and the development of a new culture. Kyoto gave occasional trouble. The retired Emperor Go-Toba tried to restore government to Kyoto but was defeated. To prevent further troubles, Kamakura deputies were stationed in Kyoto. In 1226, a new Council of State was established, and in 1232 it enacted a new legal code for the warrior class. The old ritualistic Chinese laws were replaced by laws based on social needs and common sense.

In 1333, the Kamakura shogunate came to a sudden end when two military leaders turned against the Hojo. Ashikaga no Takauji sided with the retired Emperor Go-Daigo, restoring him to the throne. Later, Nitta Yoshisada, sent by the Kamakura government to subdue Takauji, instead joined forces with him. Together they forced Hojo Takatoki and his family to commit suicide, and the Kamakura shogunate collapsed. This was not a sudden event. Takatoki had been a weak shogun, spending his time dancing and watching dog fights. Although the Kamakura government had twice driven off Mongol invasions, there was general discontent when the promised rewards for these actions were not paid. With the fall of the Kamakura shogunate, Kyoto once again became the centre of Japan's political life, to be ruled by fifteen shoguns of the Ashikaga family throughout the Muromachi period until 1568.

The Kamakura period is particularly noted for the emergence of the samurai class and Zen Buddhism. The samurai found inspiration in the teachings of Zen, which also found great favour with the Kyoto court. The samurai allegiance can be seen in the five great Zen temples at Kamakura, repeated in the *Gozan*, or five main Zen temples, in Kyoto.

Some samurai held high office under their provincial lords. The majority were the clan leader's superior soldiers, equipped with horses and good armour (Plate 6) and skilled in archery. Their way of life and prosperity depended on the power of their lord, to whom they owed absolute loyalty. At first, warrior bands (*bushidan*) were formed by local chieftains largely from their own kinsmen and kept under arms only for the duration of a particular campaign. When the fighting ended, the samurai returned home to manage their land.

By the eleventh century, the *bushidan* became larger and a new loyalty replaced kinship. Some Japanese historians have argued that this loyalty was more a commercial pact than a feudal vassalage. However, the samurai developed into a hereditary class, while the earlier bond of kinship was transformed into a fictitious relationship represented by terms such as *kenin* (houseman) and *ienoko* (child of the house), their lord with the role of father of the *bushidan*.

The samurai were not wholly occupied in fighting and throughout the Japanese provinces they were employed in a variety of official posts, those despised by the Heian courtiers. Some of the most powerful samurai settled in Kyoto, modelling their lives and their houses on the old aristocracy. They built mansions in the Shinden style, with various changes which became fashionable at this time. There were more divisions in the house, separating different functions, and the garden was on the south-western side. In smaller provincial towns, such as Kanizawa, the samurai lived in their own quarter. Today, in the Nagamachi district, one can still see a number of samurai houses, half-hidden behind earthen walls. Facing imminent defeat on the island of Shikoku, some Taira samurai fled into the mountains and settled there, in a district called Heike Mura. An elderly woman living there in an exceptionally large farmhouse claimed to be a descendant of the Taira samurai. She was a person of striking looks and dignity who may well have been descended from the Taira clan.

Reminders of the samurai's martial skills remain in Kyoto. Kendo (wooden swordsmanship) is practiced by schoolboys all over Japan. In annual festivals at the ancient Shimogamo shrine in central Kyoto, there are still horse races (Plate 7) and archery on horseback (Plate 8). At the twelfth-century temple of Sanjusangendo (Fig. 3.1), the rear of the long temple building is still used for an archery competition held each January. It requires great skill to reach the target without one's arrow touching the overhanging roof.

The development of Buddhism was important in the Kamakura period (Figs. 3.2 and 3.3), and there was an obvious

3.1 Sanjusangendo Temple (1164, rebuilt 1266).

interplay between the ethics of the military government, the samurai, the increasing popularity of the simple faith of Amida Buddhism, and the establishment of Zen Buddhism at the heart of Japanese religion and culture. The priest Honen (1133–1212) preached the faith of *nembutsu* (recitation of Amida's name) in the streets of Kyoto and founded the Jodo

3.2 Seated Buddha, gilt bronze, Kamakura period (1185–1392). Pitt Rivers Museum, Oxford.

3.3 The great bronze Buddha at Kamakura (1252).

29

or Pure Land sect. This simple faith was popular both with the court and among the people. Honen's leading disciple, Shinran (1173–1263), founded the Jodo Shin sect, a further development of Amida Buddhism. Nichiren (1222–82), another reformer reacting against the corruption of the older Buddhist sects, doubted the efficacy of Jodo teaching and eventually developed a new sect which centred on the Lotus Sutra. All three of these religious leaders suffered periods of persecution and exile, but their sects have survived until today.

Zen Buddhism had been known in the early Heian period, but it did not become established in Japan until the priest Eisai (1141–1215), founder of the Rinzai sect of Zen, returned from a second visit to China in 1191. During this visit he had spent four years studying Zen, both through meditation and the use of *koans*, the illogical sayings that free the mind, such as 'what is the sound of one hand clapping?' When Eisai returned to Japan he taught Zen in Kyushu and Kyoto. Arousing the anger of the monks on Mount Hiei, he went to Kamakura to seek the patronage of the military government.

Under the patronage of both the Kamakura shoguns and the emperors in Kyoto, the great Zen temples were established. Eisai founded Kennin-ji in Kyoto in 1202; followed by Tofuku-ji (1236); Nanzen-ji (1291) (ranked highest among the five great Zen temples); Myoshin-ji (1318); Daitoku-ji (1324); Tenryu-ji (1339); and Shokoku-ji (1392). Originally, all the great Zen temples were sited along the borders of Kyoto, but now their isolation has been obliterated by the expansion of the city and all their sites have been reduced in size. But the lives within these temples have not changed all that much since their founding. Their regime is a mixture of long hours of meditation interspersed with periods of physical labour. Once the initial period of several years' training is completed, the priests enjoy an easier life, living in the various sub-temples which cluster around the main buildings. In medieval times, when Buddhism was the dominant religion, these great temples looked after the surrounding community, providing pastoral care and, in the case of Tofuku-ji, a large public steam bath, which still exists today.

Zen Buddhism brought not only a new kind of faith to Japan, but also a complete culture ranging from painting and calligraphy to the tea ceremony. Tea had been imported from China in the Nara period (eighth century), and certain temples practised ceremonial tea drinking. Eisai brought seeds of the tea plant when he returned from China and it is said that these were planted at Kozan-ji Temple in the mountains to the north-west of Kyoto. In the Kamakura period, however, tea was only drunk by monks to help them stay awake during long periods of meditation or taken as medicine. The tea ceremony, much influenced by Zen, was not developed until the fifteenth and sixteenth centuries, by which time Zen had permeated many artistic and martial activities: painting, garden design, calligraphy, tea ceremony, swordsmanship, and archery. The intense practice of any of these activities could, in its own way, be a substitute for meditation and a path to enlightenment. It was this diversity that lent a special appeal to the samurai.

The great Zen temples built in Kyoto in the thirteenth and fourteenth centuries are evidence of the power and respect that Zen acquired, patronized by emperors and shoguns alike. They had massive gates, like Nanzen-ji, and great complexes of sub-temples clustered around the main buildings, like Daitoku-ji and Myoshin-ji, the latter with walled streets like an old town. These temples had a common layout: the gate, the hall of meditation, the main temple, and the abbot's quarters stretched out in a wood of pines. They remain the largest and most impressive temples in Kyoto.

31

Most famous today are the many and varied gardens of these temples, particularly the dry gardens of stone and sand, Zen landscapes, for meditation (Fig. 3.4). Daitoku-ji covers 56 acres and today has some twenty sub-temples, many with famous gardens. The most famous of these, and the most Zen in style, is the semi-enclosed and very small dry garden of Daisen-in. It represents in sand and carefully chosen rocks a mountainous landscape which runs down to the sea, where a rock resembling a ship sails on the raked waves of sand.

Most famous of all is the dry garden of Ryoan-ji, where five groups of rocks are enigmatically arranged in an area of carefully raked sand about the size of a tennis court, backed by an oiled clay wall. Were it not for the large crowds who flock to this garden, and the loudspeaker blaring an explanation, it would be a perfect place to meditate. Originally, these Zen gardens were reserved for the use of the monks who sat withdrawn in quiet meditation, enjoying relief from the more severe *zazen* (sitting) in the *zendo* (hall of meditation).

3.4 Zen dry garden, Nanzen-ji Temple (founded 1291).

The social changes of the Kamakura period triggered Kyoto's expansion, particularly across the Kamogawa River towards the eastern mountains. The great Zen temples were built on the outskirts of the city, to the north, west, and south, where they could find sufficient land for such large complexes. Only Eisai's Kennin-ji was near the centre. Other temples, palaces, and splendid villas began to occupy the land between the river and the mountains, while in the streets samurai swaggered with their two swords. It was probably a common sight to see Zen monks, their faces hidden by the deep half-bowl of their straw hats, begging for alms.

There is little surviving illustrative material of this period, but the thirteenth-century military romance, the *Heike Monogatari*—an account of the Minamoto and Taira struggle—gives a picture of Kyoto in the late twelfth century. After the capture of the Empress Kenreimon'in, she became a nun in the remote convent of Jakko-in, which still exists in the mountains to the north-east of Kyoto at Ohara. There is a moving description when the priestly emperor, Goshirakawa, goes to visit her in this distant place. Some thirty years ago Jakko-in and its surroundings had hardly changed from the beautiful description in this romance, with the summer grasses and the sound of the waterfall. Today, it has become a busy tourist attraction and the path across the valley is lined with souvenir shops.

For a livelier account of this great conflict, there is the fictionalized version, *The Heike Story*, written between 1950 and 1957 by the popular historical novelist, Eiji Yoshikawa. The facts are all here in a highly evocative account of Kyoto; it is written with marvellous energy and captures the relentless rivalry of the two great clans.

4

The Culture of the Ashikaga Shoguns:
The Muromachi Period 1334–1568

With the collapse of the Kamakura government, Ashikaga no Takauji decided that he could keep a tighter control over the emperor and the court if he moved his military government to Kyoto. He was appointed shogun in 1338 and from that date Japan was ruled by fifteen Ashikaga shoguns.

The Ashikaga shogunate established itself in the north of the city, in the area called Muromachi, which in turn gave its name to this period of government. The shoguns occupied various buildings, the most famous of which was a splendid palace called the Muromachi-dono, popularly called the 'Flower Palace'. It was built by the third shogun, Ashikaga no Yoshimitsu (1358–1408), but later was totally destroyed. Yoshimitsu, deeply influenced by Zen, built the great Zen temple of Shokuku-ji a little to the east of his palace. To the west lay the Ashikaga mortuary chapel in the temple of Toji-in, built by Takauji, the first shogun, who was cremated and buried there. It is uncertain where the other fourteen shoguns are buried (except for the fifth and tenth), but all their memorial tablets and their statues are preserved at Toji-in, together with its beautiful garden.

Yoshimitsu retired in 1394, and his nine-year-old son succeeded him. He then adopted the tonsure of a Zen priest and retreated to the former Saionji Kintsune estate below the north-western mountains of Kyoto. Here he built a series of sumptuous buildings, Kinkaku-ji, the Golden Pavilion, being the only one left for us to admire (Fig. 4.1). It is a replica, built after a deranged Buddhist monk burnt down the original in 1950.

4.1 Kinkaku-ji (The Golden Pavilion), Kaneko Hosui (1815–1864). Pitt Rivers Museum, Oxford.

Yoshimitsu had no real intention of retiring. He intended to live with all the prestige of a retired emperor, exercising power from behind the throne. There is no reason to doubt his sincerity in becoming a Zen priest, however. At that time, the Zen temples of Kyoto exercised great political influence, and senior priests were frequently important political advisers. Yoshimitsu's Zen priesthood added an extra dimension to his political influence.

Originally, Yoshimitsu's retreat had many elegant buildings, including two pagodas. The Golden Pavilion still shows the extravagance of Kitayama culture (Fig. 4.2). A three-storey structure, it is an architectural hybrid using Buddhist and

4.2 Kinkaku-ji (1397), The Golden Pavilion.

secular styles popular at the time. Its opulence is beautifully reflected in the large pond which spreads out before it, with rocks and small islets breaking the surface of the water.

From what remains, it is hard to imagine the luxury of this retreat, or the enormous power of the retired shogun. Nothing seems to have been beyond him. Here he entertained Emperor Go-Komatsu, the first time an emperor had stayed under the roof of a commoner. Yoshimitsu also received ambassadors from China, at which time he negotiated to his own great advantage a supply of coinage. Such occasions were organized on the most lavish scale, befitting his guests and demonstrating his own power and prestige.

Yoshimitsu was not only a clever ruler who brought a period of comparative peace to Japan, he was also a great patron of various arts, who stimulated an artistic flowering which came to be known as Kitayama culture. Yoshimitsu brought together the influences of Zen and Japanese court culture, with his own deep admiration for the Chinese art of the Sung and Yuan dynasties. Yoshimitsu also encouraged Chinese studies in the form then called 'Gozan literature'. In China, Gozan had referred to the sacred Buddhist mountains, but in Kyoto it was used to describe the five great Zen temples, where the monks produced a variety of religious and secular writings, as well as prose and poetry, always in Chinese. This literary taste was matched by an admiration for Chinese-style ink painting, seen in the work of the Shikoku monk-painter Josetsu, and the monk-painter of Tofuku-ji, Mincho. Another literary genre encouraged by Yoshimitsu was the linked verse of *renga* and *haikai*. *Renga*, a complicated sequence of short poems involving six poets or more, shows the Japanese fondness for short poems suitable for capturing experiences of nature or emotion.

Yoshimitsu also took a deep interest in architecture and gardening, as exemplified in the extravagant splendour of his own country retreat, more suitable for a retired emperor than a retired shogun. But among all his lavish patronage, nothing was more important than the development of the Noh theatre, which became his greatest passion (Plate 9).

Today, Noh plays are performed entirely by amateur actors. In the fourteenth century a less refined form of Noh was performed by wandering companies seeking patronage where they could find it, for the most part leading a threadbare existence. The main groups in the Nara and Kyoto area enjoyed the patronage of shrines and temples, and at festivals they performed religious plays and amusements. Early Noh was a more lively and popular form of entertainment, a mixture of morality plays, dancing and music, juggling and acrobatics, totally different from the slow, formalized Noh that developed later.

It was Kan'ami (1333–84), a great actor and dancer, and his son, Zeami (1363–1443), Noh's greatest playwrights, who took the raw material of the popular performance and turned it into one of the world's great theatrical forms. In 1374, when their group was performing at the Imagumano Shrine in Kyoto, Yoshimatsu was in the audience and was greatly taken by the performance. He took the company under his wing and, to the disgust of Kan'ami, the young Zeami into his bed. But he was a generous patron and gave father and son every opportunity to develop their new theatrical ideas.

Kan'ami laid the groundwork for a serious Noh theatre, through both his own plays and his outstanding talent as a performer. When Zeami died, he was about twenty-one, separated by a generation from the more popular travelling theatre which had inspired his father. Living in the world of Yoshimitsu, Zeami's work as an actor, leader of his troupe, and a playwright was deeply influenced by Zen. The forty or so plays attributed to him reflect the artistic principles of restraint and suggestion rather than direct statement. These

1. Nakajima (late Edo period), detail from a scroll painting of the Ushi Matsuri held at Koryu-ji, a temple originally belonging to the Hata family. This festival is one of the oldest in Kyoto. Pitt Rivers Museum, Oxford.

2. A village in a mountain valley, Roger Nicholson, 1982.

3. The colonnade fronting the Heian Shrine.

4. Shinsen-en garden.

5. Portrait of Minamoto no Yoritomo (late twelfth century), Jingo-ji Temple.

6. Samurai armour (late Edo period). Pitt Rivers Museum, Oxford.

7. Kansai (late Edo period), the annual horse race at the Kamigamo Shrine, Kyoto, held on 5 May. Pitt Rivers Museum, Oxford.

8. Samurai battle scene, painted *obi* (sash), nineteenth century. Pitt Rivers Museum, Oxford.

9. Noh mask (Edo period). Pitt Rivers Museum, Oxford.

10. Hideyoshi's garden at Samboin Temple (1598).

11. Panorama of Kyoto, woodblock print showing early influence of Western perspective. Kyoto, middle Edo period.

12. Replica boat and rice bales of the type formerly used for transport between central Kyoto and Fushimi port.

13. Katsura Detached Palace (1620–24), autumn richness of the garden.

14. *Kosode*, a richly embroidered type of kimono (late Edo period). Pitt Rivers Museum, Oxford.

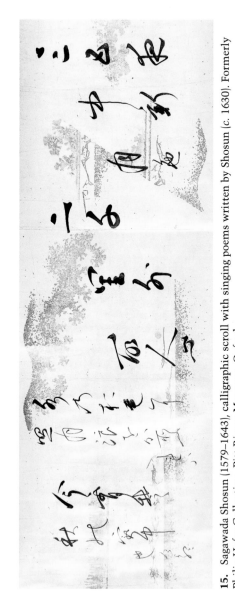

15. Sagawada Shosun (1579–1643), calligraphic scroll with singing poems written by Shosun (c. 1630). Formerly Philip Hofer Collection. Pitt Rivers Museum, Oxford.

16. Hoen (1804–67), detail from a scroll painting depicting people admiring the autumn maples at Tsutenkyo Bridge, Tofuku-ji Temple, Kyoto. Pitt Rivers Museum, Oxford.

17. A collection of incense boxes (showing the lids), for use in the tea ceremony. Japanese and Korean, modern. Pitt Rivers Museum, Oxford.

18. Keisai Eisen, woodblock print from a series, *48 Grains of the Floating World* (1820–30). Author's collection.

19. A Kyoto *surimono* depicting bean throwing (Setsubun) in February, to mark the coming of spring. Author's collection.

20. Clifton Karhu, *Kyoto roofscape*, cotton furoshiki, modern. Pitt Rivers Museum, Oxford.

plays, still popular, and his many essays on the nature of Noh, continue to be the foundation of all Noh theatre. The plays and performances of Kan'ami and Zeami must have been among the highlights of the Kitayama arts, and the period's most important bequest to Japanese culture.

Ashikaga no Yoshimitsu died in 1408. He was an important patron of Japanese art and culture, and despite his retirement to the Golden Pavilion, he remained a shrewd and effective ruler, furthering both his personal interests and those of Japan. His shogunate was a period of stability and prosperity for Kyoto, during which he maintained the balance between the rule of the capital and the necessary support of its vassals, the provincial warlords.

He bequeathed the Golden Pavilion to his great Zen foundation, Shokuku-ji. According to his wishes, his magnificent villa was converted to a Zen temple, with the great Zen master, Muso Soseki (1275–1351), as its posthumous honorary abbot. The Golden Pavilion is still administered by Shokoku-ji.

By the middle of the fifteenth century, Yoshimitsu's golden age was disintegrating into the most disastrous period of Kyoto's history. His grandson, Ashikaga no Yoshimasa (1435–90), became the eighth Ashikaga shogun in 1449. He was a weak man, not interested in government, who preferred to devote himself to the arts. It is said that his wife and his concubines decided the affairs of state.

When Yoshimasa failed to have a son and heir, he named his brother, Yoshimi, as his successor, but tried to cancel this arrangement when his wife gave him an heir, Yoshihisa. This immediately led to a dispute over the succession, these quarrels within the shogunate set against a time of extreme political unrest and rioting in Kyoto. Yoshimasa had failed to check the powers of the provincial lords, and when the succession dispute led to fighting in the capital, the powerful families took sides to protect their own interests. The terrible Onin War raged within the capital from 1467 to 1477, bringing ten years of pillage and indiscriminate destruction. Although the question of the succession was settled in 1473, the war, like a madness, raged on for another four years. The Kyoto of the Muromachi and previous periods was largely burnt to the ground.

While Kyoto continued to burn, with appalling suffering among its population, Yoshimasa, displaying an extraordinary lack of responsibility, abdicated on 7 January 1474 in favour of his son Yoshihisa. He retired to Higashiyama, the eastern mountains, where he built a series of handsome buildings centred on Ginkaku-ji, the Silver Pavilion (never actually silvered) (Fig. 4.3), turning his back on the smouldering remains of Kyoto across the river. Unlike his grandfather, he forsook all political activity, but, like Yoshimitsu, he devoted himself to various Japanese arts, creating what was to be called Higashiyama culture, hardly less important than the culture of the Golden Pavilion and, like Kitayama culture, heavily influenced by Zen. From what was a much larger complex, only the Silver Pavilion, the Togu-do (Yoshimasa's residence), and the beautiful gardens remain.

Yoshimasa took over the site of a former Tendai monastery, a perfect place set against the eastern hills of Kyoto. Today, it is not a long walk from the centre of Kyoto, but it was east of the Kamogawa River, still considered remote countryside at that time. Yoshimasa had neither the power nor the wealth of his grandfather, and his country retreat was built on a smaller and more restrained scale than the sumptuous Golden Pavilion. Ginkaku-ji, the Silver Pavilion, is in no way ostentatious, but it is built in a most elegant and perfectly proportioned style. Originally the Kannon Hall, Ginkaku-ji is a two-storey building with a

4.3 Ginkaku-ji (1482), The Silver Pavilion.

shoin-style meditation hall below and a chapel for a gilt Kannon figure above. Yoshimasa took holy orders in 1485, and once again the links with Shokoku-ji were important in both religion and art. In front of the Silver Pavilion is a moon-viewing garden with a large raised expanse of raked white sand, called the Sea of Silver Sand, which appears to ripple in the moonlight. Near the Silver Pavilion is a large, truncated cone of sand, which also reflects the moonlight. Zen embraced the practice of moon viewing, and with a typical Zen contradiction, took equal pleasure in moonless nights. This dry garden runs along the front of the Hondo, rebuilt in the seventeenth century, and the Togu-do, the only other building remaining from the original complex.

The Togu-do, built in 1487, is a simple building with a thatched roof and contains four rooms. Traditionally, Yoshimasa occupied the eight-mat front room, the largest in the building, a simple residence for a retired shogun. At the north-eastern corner of this building is the celebrated Dojin-sai, 'Friendly Abstinence', a small, four-and-a-half mat room which became the traditional size for the Japanese tea ceremony, only seating the tea master and four or five guests. Yoshimasa was a patron and follower of the way of tea and its development at the Silver Pavilion under the guidance of his tea master, the priest Murata Shuko. He laid the foundations of the tea ceremony, with strong Zen overtones, which became formalized by Sen no Rikyu a hundred years later, basically in the form still practised today.

The main garden of the Silver Pavilion surrounds a long pond, with Crane and Turtle islands, and a stroll garden, its paths winding among fine rocks, trees, azaleas, and soft patches of moss. The paths lead up the mountainside, at the highest point offering a fine view of the Silver Pavilion across the garden. This scene is at its most beautiful rich with autumn colours. It is strange to think of Yoshimasa enjoying this peaceful landscape with war raging little more than three miles away.

Apart from tea, Yoshimasa patronized literature, scholarship, and painting much as Yoshimitsu had done. Scholars were encouraged to study the classics, Noh drama developed and poets practised linked-verse poetry. The production of fine lacquer and other materials to provide implements for the tea ceremony gave stimulus to local craftsmanship, all of this making the Silver Pavilion a centre of artistic activity which attracted men of all classes.

In Yoshimasa's patronage of painting, his links with Shokoku-ji are clear. The great Zen temple had become an important artistic centre in its own right, particularly as a training ground for painters, some of whom were to become the most influential of their time. This tradition lives on: once a year a special service is held when the walls are hung, scroll touching scroll, with the temple's collection, a breathtaking display of masterpieces by famous artists who had worked at the temple.

In Yoshimasa's day, Chinese Ming ink paintings were highly admired, particularly this Chinese style as interpreted by the Japanese painters Shobun and Sesshu Toyo, both more closely associated with Shokoku-ji than with the Silver Pavilion. Shobun was a monk-painter at the Zen temple, where Sesshu became his pupil. But their styles, and this new Kyoto school of painting, were deeply admired by Yoshimasa, who must have encouraged its practice among his own artists. Chinese art was still influential, from its craggy landscapes to the design of implements for the tea ceremony.

Against the background of the Golden Pavilion and the Silver Pavilion—retreats for two rulers of Kyoto—the position of the emperor and the court diminished, even petrified, while life for the ordinary people of Kyoto must have grown more miserable. Worse was to come for the capital. Although the Onin War officially ended in 1477, the powerful daimyos (fuedal lords) of the provinces had successfully flexed their muscles and tasted power; Kyoto remained the centre of an intermittent civil war for the next hundred years. Yoshimasa died in 1490 and, following his grandfather's example, he bequeathed the Silver Pavilion to Shokoku-ji, again for conversion to a Zen temple.

5

The Reconstruction of Kyoto:
The Azuchi–Momoyama Period 1568–1600

By the beginning of the sixteenth century, the centre of Kyoto had been reduced to ruins by the Onin War and the city's power weakened by the fighting among the provincial lords. The failure of the central government to unify Japan had diminished the emperor's power and rendered the last of the Ashikaga shoguns an ineffective ruler. When St Francis Xavier arrived in Kyoto, in the middle of the century, he wrote a famous letter describing the desolation of the capital. It was the lowest moment in the history of Kyoto and it took three remarkable Japanese to restore its fortunes and finally unite the country. These were the brilliant general, Oda Nobunaga (1532–82); his successor, Toyotomi Hideyoshi (1536–98); and the first Tokugawa shogun, Ieyasu (1543–1616).

Nobunaga was the son of a military governor in the region of Nagoya, in the modern prefecture of Aichi. His father had begun the process of unifying the area, and after his death Nobunaga completed his work. Driving out the last of the Ashikagas in 1573, his local military successes established his reputation and he was summoned to the capital in 1568. By military campaigns and subterfuge, he subdued more and more of the provinces and went a long way in unifying Japan. He was a ruthless general and ruler: when the nobility of northern Kyoto refused to pay the taxes he had imposed to pay for the reconstruction of southern Kyoto, he retaliated by burning down a large section of northern Kyoto. To punish the Tendai sect priests who opposed his rule, he burnt down their temples on Mount Hiei. He nursed the ambition to become the ruler of Japan but, despite his military victories and his administrative success, he made some bitter enemies. Nobunaga fell out with one of his best generals, Akechi Mitsuhide, when a plot of Nobunaga's caused the death of Mitsuhide's mother. Mitsuhide swore vengeance and his troops surrounded Nobunaga's headquarters in the Honnoji Temple in Kyoto, where Nobunaga committed suicide.

Toyotomi Hideyoshi, an outstanding general of humble birth, inherited the mantle of Nobunaga, continuing his work of unifying Japan but devoting much of his energy to the replanning and reconstruction of Kyoto. Like Nobunaga, he was ambitious to receive imperial recognition as ruler of Japan. To gain the emperor's favour he rebuilt many temples and built the Sento Palace. In all his work of reconstruction, Hideyoshi worked to an overall plan which would improve the layout of Kyoto, increase its security, and, by creating districts for various Buddhist sects, help to keep the priestly population under control. The Kyoto we see today, though there have been many changes since 1600, is in its basic layout the replanned city of Hideyoshi, built over the skeleton of the avenues and streets of Heian-kyo.

One of the greatest leaders in Japanese history, Hideyoshi was a man of genius. He was a brilliant soldier, an inspired and far-sighted administrator, and a great patron of the arts, above all the tea ceremony. While his first task was to restore Kyoto and to make it a more modern and efficient city, Hideyoshi's ambitions were boundless. His humble birth forbade him from ever becoming shogun, but his power was evident in his domestic campaigns, his attempt to conquer Korea and China, his castle-mansions where he entertained the emperor, his flamboyant patronage of the arts, the richly painted decorations and carving for his castle-mansions, and the open-air tea ceremonies for hundreds of guests.

His power enabled him to command vast quantities of materials and labour, both for his own building schemes and for the reconstruction of Kyoto. In only sixteen years of power, he had built a moated wall around Kyoto and a network of narrow streets, intended to check rioting. In the same period, he built Osaka Castle for his personal use, the great mansion of Jurakudai in central Kyoto, a further castle-mansion to the south of the city at Fushimi, the great but ill-fated bronze Buddha at the Hokoji Temple, and Samboin, whose garden is one of the most elaborate in Kyoto (Plate 10). This frantic building programme must have placed a great burden on the population of Kyoto, straining the resources of the now subdued provincial daimyo, and was at this time that the merchants of the city began to flourish.

Hideyoshi was not only concerned with the enemy without, he was also determined to control the priestly power within the city, which had caused such disturbance in the past. Whereas Nobunaga had dealt with the old threat of Mount Hiei, Hideyoshi isolated the most powerful Buddhist sects within the city's boundaries. The Jodo sect were forced to build their temples along the boundaries of Teramachi street, and the Nichiren sect were confined to the northern part of the city, Teranouchi. The Nichiren sect later left Kyoto, but Hideyoshi's Jodo 'ghetto' can still be seen today in Teramachi-dori, 'the street of temples', which runs north to south all the way from Kitaoji-dori to Gojo-dori. Even now, this street is lined with temple gateways, though few are open to visitors. Behind the temples to the east are large burial grounds, hidden from the street, which suggest that these temples were once larger and grander. Today, only Rozan-ji Temple is noteworthy, with a fine garden. However, the whole ensemble of temples stretching down Teramachi-dori remains an interesting monument to Hideyoshi's careful town planning.

Hideyoshi's was the age of castle building. The days of temporary fortifications were eclipsed by the introduction of gunpowder, purchased from the Portuguese merchants in Nagasaki. Some of the castles, like Hideyoshi's Osaka Castle, completed in 1585, were massively fortified stone structures, built primarily to withstand a siege. Other castles were primarily princely dwellings, like Hideyoshi's last castle, built in Fushimi in the south of Kyoto. In between were castle-mansions like the lavish Jurakudai, which Hideyoshi built somewhere in the neighbourhood of Nijo but then dismantled only eight years after it was completed. It seems likely that this grand residence, with a wall and other features of castle architecture, was mainly built to entertain the emperor and thereby to increase Hideyoshi's prestige. The emperor was so impressed with his hospitality that he extended his stay from three to five days.

Richard Ponsonby Fane, in his book *Kyoto*, quotes from an old document a description of Hideyoshi's first arrival at Jurakudai, which gives some idea of the splendour of his lifestyle and the attention he attracted in the capital:

The dwelling house was surrounded by a stone wall . . . the pillars were of iron and the doors of copper. . . . The pattern of the tiles was like jewelled tigers breathing in the wind, and like golden dragons intoning in the clouds. When it was finished in 1587, Hideyoshi moved thither from Osaka Castle. He arrived at Yodo with several hundred vessels coated with gold and silver. . . . From Yodo, with 500 carriages and 5,000 coolies, he arrived at the capital. The court nobles and feudal lords came to meet him and all the way the thoroughfare was crowded with people.

This was also an age of military rulers, whose tastes in art and decoration did not follow the more restrained styles favoured by the court and Zen aesthetic principles. The great castles of this period included great domestic halls which required large painted screens and other decoration. Great birds and gnarled pine trees symbolized more manly tastes, painted in strong, rich colours to stand out against the gold backgrounds. This style is typified in the work of Kano Eitoku (1543–90), who painted screens for both Nobunaga and Hideyoshi.

Unfortunately, none of Hideyoshi's castles remains. Jurakudai was dismantled at his orders, and Fushimi Castle was destroyed by an earthquake early in the seventeenth century, about the same time that Osaka Castle was demolished. While the castles one sees today at Fushimi and Osaka are modern reproductions, gateways, other architectural features, and whole rooms of screen paintings were given to various temples in Kyoto and have been incorporated into their structures. The most often quoted example is the huge temple of Nishi-Honganji, which was built on its present site in 1591 on Hideyoshi's orders, and later received whole painted rooms from Fushimi and the beautiful *Floating Cloud Pavilion* from Jurakudai. Birth may have prevented Hideyoshi from becoming shogun or emperor, but these remains of his castles' domestic quarters show that his standard of living was probably far higher than that of the contemporary emperor.

Hideyoshi's order to rebuild the temples and the removal of others to his chosen part of the city was part of Kyoto's tradition. The Japanese have long been master carpenters, and within a few years of the founding of the capital, they would have been kept busy repairing or replacing the palaces and temples of Kyoto destroyed or damaged by fire, earthquakes, and other destructive forces. Large temples were not only rebuilt but, for a variety of reasons, were frequently moved to another site, often a considerable distance away. This tradition of architectural flux may partly explain how Hideyoshi was able to organize the reconstruction of Kyoto so quickly.

The extent to which Hideyoshi was personally interested in such Japanese arts as tea ceremony and flower arrangement is uncertain, but there is no doubt that he liked to enlarge his prestige by spectacular events, like the historic tea ceremony he organized at the Kitano Shrine in 1587. He had inherited a great tea master, Rikyu (1522–91), from Nobunaga. Rikyu's grandfather had been a tea master in the service of Ashikaga Yoshimasa, and though his family became wealthy merchants dealing in fish, Rikyu studied tea ceremony under various masters and also studied Zen at the great temple of Daitoku-ji in northern Kyoto. In their earlier relations, Rikyu enjoyed the favour of Hideyoshi, who gave him considerable land. It was Rikyu who performed the luxurious tea ceremony at the Imperial Palace in 1585, organized by Hideyoshi to further his ties with the emperor. There is no doubt that Hideyoshi admired Rikyu and the new ideas with which he changed the tea ceremony. Rikyu gave it a basic form which has survived until today as the generally accepted way of tea, both in the utensils used and the spirit in which the ceremony is performed. He preferred the simplest of utensils, writing that 'the tea ceremony is nothing more than boiling water, steeping the tea, and drinking it'. In his search for simplicity and a rustic atmosphere, he reduced the size of the teahouse to only two tatami mats. At this time, the tea ceremony was only for men, rooted in Zen and the warrior lifestyle, and women were not allowed to perform the ceremony until the mid-eighteenth century (Figs. 5.1 and 5.2).

In 1591, for some unknown reason, Rikyu fell into disfavour with Hideyoshi, who ordered him to commit suicide. Unlike many of Japan's generals, Hideyoshi was not normally a vindictive man, and the reason for Rikyu's death has remained a mystery, one which has spawned both novels and films. We do know that he most unwisely set up a

5.1 Cake bowl in the form of a water-pourer, attributed to the Rokubei family of potters (late Edo period). Pitt Rivers Museum, Oxford.

5.2 Tea bowl decorated with a crane, red raku ware (late Edo period).

life-size statue of himself in the main gate of Daitoku-ji. Hideyoshi, always sensitive about his own prestige, may have taken this as an act of insufferable arrogance from a man who was already becoming too important. Other suggested reasons include the possibility that Rikyu refused to give his daughter to Hideyoshi, or more simply that he was demanding too high a price for his tea wares. Whatever the real reason, the enigmatic suicide of this great tea master has only served to increase the interest in Rikyu ever since. He gave the tea ceremony a new prominence and today the Ura Senke Foundation, headed by Rikyu's direct descendant, promotes the tea ceremony all over the world, with thousands of members in Japan. Despite all the modernization of Japanese life, the way of tea flourishes.

Of the few remaining monuments in Kyoto which recall the power and tastes of Hideyoshi, none is more perfect or more evocative of the Momoyama period than the magnificent garden he had created at Samboin Temple (Plate 10), part of the complex that centres on the far older pagoda of Daigoji. The area was renowned for its cherry trees and in the spring of 1598 Hideyoshi went there to enjoy the cherry blossoms, making camp on 'flower-viewing hill', close to the dilapidated temple of Samboin.

According to history, or legend, Giyen, the priest at Samboin, begged Hideyoshi to restore his temple. Hideyoshi saw the possibilities and the work of restoration began immediately. The buildings that exist today are of the Momoyama period, with some later alterations. According to Ponsonby Fane, some parts of the temple came from Fushimi Castle. But the main interest is the garden which fronts the Sen-den, the construction of which is said to have been carried out under the personal supervision of Hideyoshi. One important feature of the garden is the wealth of fine stones. These, it is said, were extracted by Hideyoshi from various feudal lords, and some from the garden of Jurakudai.

It is a beautiful garden, as sumptuous in its horticultural way as the decoration of Hideyoshi's castle-mansions. A large pond spreads before the verandas of the temple, the water broken up by small islands joined by variously designed bridges. Everywhere are magnificent rocks, trees, and shrubs, the main island crowned by a flat-topped pine, trained over a bamboo trellis. It is one of the richest gardens in Kyoto, and perhaps the only one where photography is forbidden without advance permission. When permission has been granted, the priest hangs a heavy wooden board around the photographer's neck, announcing that he is allowed to photograph, although the board is so cumbersome that it makes raising a camera to the eye difficult.

5.3 Sanjo-bashi Bridge (1590).

Looking again at this magnificent garden and the variety of pavilions that overlook it, it seems likely that Hideyoshi was creating a suitable setting for the ostentatious parties he loved to give rather than founding a new temple. While Samboin is now his finest monument left in Kyoto, one which has outlasted his great castles and their grand interiors, it would be foolish to pretend that Hideyoshi left a recognizable mark on Kyoto that has survived the process of change and modernization. There are individual features, like Teramachi-dori, and his great central bridge, Sanjo-bashi (Fig. 5.3), which originally marked one end of the official road from Edo (Tokyo), called the Tokaido, that became the main thoroughfare of Japan in the following period. Hideyoshi is buried on top of a steep hill opposite his Hoko-ji Temple and his shrine, Hokoku. A long flight of stone steps lead to his tomb at the top of the steep slope of the Amidagamine hill. It is surprisingly simple for such a great and powerful man, but the site does command a marvellous view over the city which occupied so much of his life.

6

The Rise of the Merchant Class:
The Edo Period 1600–1868

After Hideyoshi's death, Tokugawa Ieyasu (1542–1616), a former general with both Nobunaga and Hideyoshi, seized power. In 1603 he was appointed shogun by the emperor and, suspicious of courtly and priestly influences in Kyoto, established his government in his castle at Edo, later to become Tokyo. Like his two predecessors, he was a good soldier and a skillful politician. He completed the unification of Japan, disposed of Hideyoshi's descendants, and subdued the provincial warlords. The enfeebled emperors and their court continued in Kyoto, carefully supervised by officials from Edo, distracted by the shogun's permission to build new villas and gardens. By his death, Ieyasu had established his family's power and they were to rule Japan until the Meiji restoration in 1868.

When the first Europeans and Jesuit missionaries landed in Japan in 1543, Japan was subject to foreign influences other than those of China and Korea for the first time. Many Japanese became Christians, the new influences were absorbed without friction, and a Christian church was built in Kyoto. When the Dominican missionaries arrived, however, they sought to undermine their Jesuit rivals by reporting to the government that they were little more than spies. Hideyoshi started the persecution of Christians, and by 1637 the Catholic missionaries were driven out of Japan. After that only the Dutch were allowed to maintain a tiny trading post on Decima, an artificial island in the harbour of Nagasaki, where the Chinese were also allowed to continue minimal trading. In effect, Japan was from this date isolated from the rest of the world until 1868; a medieval country devoid of modernization.

The Tokugawa government, in an attempt to exercise control over everything, became intensely bureaucratic. To give a kind of respectability to their exercise of power, they encouraged scholars to develop neo-Confucianism, which gave a moral justification to their draconian laws and tight organization of society. Under this regime, responsibility lay with the organization or group to which one belonged, giving the group the right to interfere with individual liberty and to spy on everyone. By the middle of the eighteenth century there was a network of spies in cities like Kyoto, often depicted as shakuhachi (bamboo flute) players, disguised by large baskets covering their heads. The constrictions on all members of Japanese society went as far as to legislate the colour of umbrellas, for example, blue for Confucian scholars.

Tokugawa society was divided and stratified into rigid classes, each with its own responsibilities and duties to society. This class system—caste system might be a more accurate description—was headed by the samurai who had a duty to set an example of honourable behaviour to the rest of society. Below them came the farmers, deserving of this rank because they produced the food on which the whole of society depended. There was little honour in their position, as their way of life was hard and mostly miserable. Indeed, under the great landowners, the farmer's life was little more than slavery.

These classes were defined in light of what each section of society contributed, and hence the craftsmen were ranked above the merchants, who were regarded as men only concerned with increasing their own wealth. The government was probably nervous of the growing power that wealth brought to the merchant class, and its fears were justified.

Wealth was to tumble the carefully constructed social system. Increasingly, the samurai had no real function in a peaceful Japan, and no way of earning a living. They began to look enviously at the prosperous merchants, first for loans, and later, perhaps to repay the debt, for marriage into a merchant family. This not only weakened the class system, but led to the samurai going into trade. In Edo, Osaka, and Kyoto, the successful merchants began to ignore the imposed class barriers and to create their own way of life and a new culture which appealed to their tastes.

By the early eighteenth century, Kyoto, despite Tokugawa restrictions, became a city of merchants. Their activities, their shops, and their popular festivals (Fig. 6.1) are beautifully depicted in many screens, golden clouds floating

6.1 The Gion Matsuri (1–29 July), Kyoto's greatest festival, seen here depicted in an eighteenth-century screen.

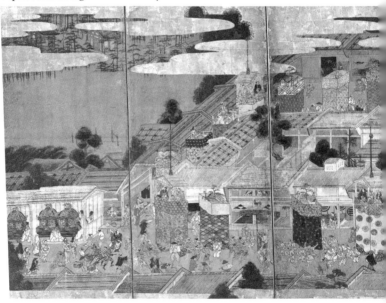

over their prosperous way of life. The great temples line the horizon but imperial palaces and courtiers' mansions are absent. This is a commercial city where life vibrates in the streets (Plate 11). There were similar scenes in Edo and Osaka. It became the age of the merchant, the new patron of art; the theatre, the 'floating world' illustrated in woodblock prints, and the life of the geisha quarters all flourished.

Although Kyoto was encircled by rivers, it was a long way from the sea and the port of Osaka. By the beginning of the seventeenth century, the Hozu and Kamo rivers were beginning to be dredged to allow river traffic. A little later, with the excavation of a canal running from the centre of Kyoto to the Ujigawa River, a more direct waterway to Osaka was created, and passengers and freight changed from small

flat-bottomed boats to larger ones at Fushimi port, south of the city. The canal still exists in the area south of the Fujita Hotel, where a replica boat of the Edo period is moored with a cargo of rice bales (Plate 12). There is a small museum in Fushimi illustrating the old waterway, which still runs traditional passenger boats down the river to Osaka. All these improvements to Kyoto's waterways were paid for by rich merchant families, proving that such wealthy merchant houses already existed in the early seventeenth century.

Kyoto continued to spread, with a growing population prompting a great increase in the number of domestic dwellings. Many smaller merchant families lived behind or above their shops and showrooms. The typical Kyoto dwelling comprised the 'eel beds', a name reflecting the way the rooms were laid out end-to-end on an elongated site little wider than the individual rooms. A long, stone-paved passage containing the kitchen ran to one side through the house, all the rooms opening onto it. The first room at the back was for entertaining guests and was used to display works of art and objects of popular culture. The next room, for family use, combined the living and dining room. These domestic quarters were separated from the front room—usually the shop facing onto the street—by a hallway that often enclosed a small garden. Usually there was a second floor which might have been used by the family or for storage. Such Kyoto houses are rapidly disappearing, though their traditional layout is echoed in the plans of some small, modern apartments.

Although the government of Japan was moved to Edo, Kyoto remained the cultural, artistic, and religious centre of the country. The rich merchants were enthusiastic patrons of the arts: architecture, gardens (Plate 13), painting, ceramics, and fine textiles (Plate 14). The court and the rich merchants patronized contemporary Kyoto artists, notably the Rimpa school, led by Sotatsu and Koetsu in the earlier seventeenth century, and by Korin in the early eighteenth century. The school's decorative but delicate style of painting, enriched with gold and silver and popular for the decoration of screens, album pages, and fans, took subjects from medieval history and from nature. Koetsu was a versatile artist, admired for his calligraphy, pottery, lacquer, and metal designs (Plate 15). Favoured by Ieyasu, he was given some land in north-western Kyoto at Takagamine, where he was joined by a group of Kyoto craftsmen, whose work became famous for its fine designs. Koetsu was best known for his calligraphic work and his decorated books, done, it is said, on paper designed by Sotatsu. His house and garden were turned into a temple, Koetsu-ji, which can be visited. The garden is famous for the graceful curving bamboo fence he designed, which later was often used as a decorative feature on textiles.

Kyoto was famous for its richly decorated textiles, mostly for kimonos (Plate 14), which were produced in the large quarter of Nishijin. Even today, though this weaving industry has much diminished, walking through the back streets of Nishijin, one can still hear the rattle of looms where the weavers work in their homes. At its height, this was one of the most prosperous merchant quarters and Kyoto kimonos (Plate 16) were in demand all over Japan. It was so wealthy that it could support its own geisha quarter, just by the Kitano Shrine, but today there are hardly enough geisha to perform the spring and autumn dances.

At the other end of Kyoto, to the south-west, was the traditional ceramic quarter, just below the ancient temple of Kiyomizu-dera, which produced both wares for the rich and souvenirs for the pilgrims visiting the temple. Now it is little more than a tourist area with many shops selling a variety of ceramics, and the fine porcelains of the seventeenth century have long gone. Tradition continues, however, in the many shops along Gojo-dori (Plate 17) that sell more useful wares, and in the annual pottery fair held on Gojo's pavements in early August.

Kyoto remains a city of traditional crafts, though some now struggle to survive. The streets of central Kyoto in the Edo period must have been lined with small shops selling the craft objects which at that time were necessities of life: fans, combs, hair ornaments, braided cords, and a variety of ceramics and implements needed to prepare Japanese food. Kyoto has long boasted of its special cuisine and even today, in the narrow street Nishiki-koji, there are many small shops selling special Kyoto foods. The sake brewers in Fushimi, to the south of the city, also became well established in the Edo period.

With their increasing wealth, the merchants wanted entertainment and this led directly to the development of the kabuki theatre, a more popular form of entertainment than the aristocratic Noh plays. It is said that kabuki grew out of the popular dances women of doubtful reputation first performed on the dry banks of the Kamogawa River. It can hardly be a coincidence that Kyoto's only surviving kabuki theatre stands near this spot.

Governments tend to regard theatres as places of immorality and sedition. The Tokugawa government was no exception and soon began to place restrictions on the kabuki actors. Soon women, a source of licentiousness, were forbidden to act. They were replaced by boys who aroused different but equally undesirable emotions in the audience. Typical of the Tokugawa attention to detail, the boys were compelled to shave the front of their hair in an attempt to make them less attractive. Restrictions on theatrical performances became so severe that in the early eighteenth century, the playwright Chikamatsu (1653–1724)—Japan's

Shakespeare—wrote all his great plays for the puppet theatre, later known as *bunraku*. By the nineteenth century it became an independent form of theatre with its own traditions.

The modern kabuki theatres of big cities like Tokyo and Kyoto are much larger than the theatres of the Edo period. Only one early nineteenth-century kabuki theatre has survived, perfectly restored and in regular use for its summer season, attracting the best actors in Japan and allowing the audience to enjoy the more intimate character of Edo kabuki. The Kanamaru-za was built close to the great pilgrimage shrine of Kompira on Shikoku Island for the entertainment of the pilgrims. After years of being a cinema and further neglect, it was moved to a better site and everything, including its man-powered stage machinery, was put back into working order. In the performance, the most noticeable difference is the close relationship between the actors and the audience, with the leading actor even throwing in a few local references. At Kanamaru-za it is easy to understand why these plays were so popular with the merchant audience, as the subjects of the plays often touched their own lives.

It was also the patronage of the rich merchants which led to the creation of Kyoto's geisha quarters and the ritualized entertainment of these highly trained women (Plate 18). In the earlier Edo period there were around seven geisha quarters in Kyoto, though in their earlier foundation there was some confusion between the courtesans of Shimabara, the licensed pleasure quarter, and the geisha, who were not supposed to offer sexual services. Today there are only three geisha quarters in Kyoto: the largest, Gion; the small but prestigious Pontocho, just across the river; and the lesser-known and diminishing quarter by the Kitano shrine.

Gion remains the largest geisha quarter, though today much of it is taken up by art dealers, restaurants, small nightclubs, and modern seven-storey buildings crammed with dozens of tiny bars. A fragment of Kyoto's past is preserved in Gion: facing the small Shirakawa River is a line of old wooden houses, their windows shaded with woven bamboo blinds, where geisha used to live in *okiya*, the homes from which they set out to entertain parties in approved restaurants. Bookings were made through the *kemban*, the local organizing office. Then as now, this office would know and approve the clients. Today, one must be a rich man to give a party with the best geisha of Gion.

Shimabara, the more popular pleasure quarter of Kyoto, had existed in the sixteenth century but was moved to the south-west of Kyoto to clear the site for Nijo Castle (Fig. 6.2). In the government's view, prostitutes, like actors, were flashpoints and Shimabara was carefully controlled. The quarter was enclosed by a wall and supervised by the police and, probably, spies. It would be wrong to describe it as a red-light district since, like the Geisha quarters, it could offer sophisticated entertainment by the *tayu*, the top courtesans,

6.2 Nijo Castle (1603), the elaborate decoration of a doorway.

62

for those who could afford their services. When prostitution was made illegal in 1958, Shimabara was closed, and only the eastern gate and two buildings remain as monuments to the pleasure quarter. The *tayu* are remembered in a procession, the *Dochu*, held on the third Sunday of April at Josho-ji Temple in northern Kyoto, long associated with the *tayu*. They wear a distinctive costume and *geta* (high wooden sandals). This glimpse of Shimabara's past reminds visitors that it had its own gorgeous style, hierarchy, and ceremony.

The pleasures of the geisha quarters gave rise to that famous Japanese feeling of fleeting pleasure, summed up in the phrase 'the floating world'. It was a hedonistic philosophy which inspired new genres of literature, poetry, drama, and, most famously, the depiction of that world in the delicate woodblock prints of the later eighteenth and early nineteenth centuries. Originally, these prints were a popular form of art, sold for a tiny price, many of them little more than advertisements for famous kabuki actors or popular courtesans. Strangely, the vast majority of these prints were produced in Edo and not in Kyoto, though they must have circulated in both cities. Kyoto produced some prints of views of the city, showing the first influence in Japanese art of Western perspective, and the charming *surimono*. Accompanied by poems, *surimono* were the collaboration of Kyoto artists and writers and were produced for literary clubs in Kyoto, often as greetings cards for the New Year or other occasions (Plate 19).

It must be obvious to the modern visitor that little remains of old Kyoto, of the Edo or any other period. Each year modernization of the city gathers pace. The court added its own new palaces and gardens in the early Edo period: the Katsura Detached Palace, with perhaps the finest landscape garden in Kyoto (Plate 13), was closely followed by the Imperial Shugakuin garden and pavilions. With a new stability, many temples were repaired and reconstructed, having been constantly damaged by fires and other disasters. Despite everything, it takes months of intensive sightseeing to see all the remains of Kyoto's past and from them to piece together the history of this great city (Plate 20).

Selected Bibliography

History

Dunn, Charles J., *Everyday Life in Traditional Japan*, Tokyo: Tuttle, 1981.

Ishikawa Tadashi, *Palaces of Kyoto*, Tokyo: Kodansha, 1977.

Iwao Seiichi, *Biographical Dictionary of Japanese History*, Tokyo: Kodansha, 1982.

Izumoji Yoshikazu, *Kyoto*, Osaka: Hoikusha, 1983.

Mosher, Gouverneur, *Kyoto, A Contemplative Guide*, Tokyo: Tuttle, 1978.

Plutschow, Herbert E., *Historical Kyoto*, Tokyo: Japan Times, 1983.

Ponsonby Fane, R., *Kyoto, The Old Capital of Japan*, privately printed: Kyoto, 1956.

———, *The Imperial House of Japan*, privately printed: Kyoto, 1959.

———, *Sovereign and Subject*, privately printed: Kyoto, 1962.

Ward, Philip, *Japanese Capitals*, Cambridge: Oleander Press, 1985.

General

Kodansha Encyclopaedia of Japan, 9 vols, Tokyo: Kodansha, 1983.

Lowe, John, *Into Japan*, London: John Murray, 1985.

———, *Glimpses of Kyoto Life*, Oxford: Pitt Rivers Museum, 1996.

Guidebooks

Cooper, Michael, *Exploring Kamakura*, Tokyo: Weatherhill, 1983.

Durston, Diane, *Old Kyoto*, Tokyo: Kodansha, 1987.

———, *Kyoto, Seven Paths to the Heart of the City*, Kyoto: Mitsumura Suiko, 1987.

Japan National Tourist Organization, *Japan, The New Official Guide*, Tokyo: Japan Travel Bureau, 1991.

Kyoto, Kyoto: Kyoto City Tourist Association, 1982.

Kyoto, Nara, Osaka, Kobe, Tokyo: Japan Travel Bureau, 1982.

Kyoto-Osaka, A Bilingual Atlas, Tokyo: Kodansha, 1992.

Martin, J. & P., *Kyoto, A Cultural Guide*, Tokyo: Tuttle, 1994.

Must-See in Kyoto, Tokyo: Japan Travel Bureau, 1985.

Nissan Guide to Kyoto & Environs, n.p.: Nissan, 1986.

Usui Shiro, *A Pilgrim's Guide to Forty-Six Temples*, Tokyo: Weatherhill, 1990.

Art and Architecture

Lowe, John, *Japanese Crafts*, London: John Murray, 1983.

Nishi, K. and K. Hozumi, *What is Japanese Architecture?*, Tokyo: Kodansha, 1985.

Paine, R. T. & A. Soper, *The Art & Architecture of Japan*, New York: Pelican History of Art, 1975.

Literature

Albery, Nobuko, *The House of Kanze*, New York: Simon & Schuster, 1985.

Aston, W. G., *A History of Japanese Literature*, Tokyo: Tuttle, 1981.

Kawabata, Y., *Beauty and Sadness*, Tokyo: Tuttle, 1991.

———, *The Old Capital*, Tokyo: Tuttle, 1991.

Mishima, Y., *The Temple of the Golden Pavilion*, London: Penguin, 1987.

Morris, Ivan, *The World of the Shining Prince*, Tokyo: Tuttle, 1978.

Murasaki Shikibu, *The Tale of Genji*, 2 vols, translated by E. G. Seidensticker, Tokyo: Tuttle ,1976.

Sei Shonagon, *The Pillow Book*, translated by Ivan Morris, London: Penguin, 1971.

Yoshikawa Eiji, *The Heike Story*, Tokyo: Tuttle, 1988.

Index

INDEX